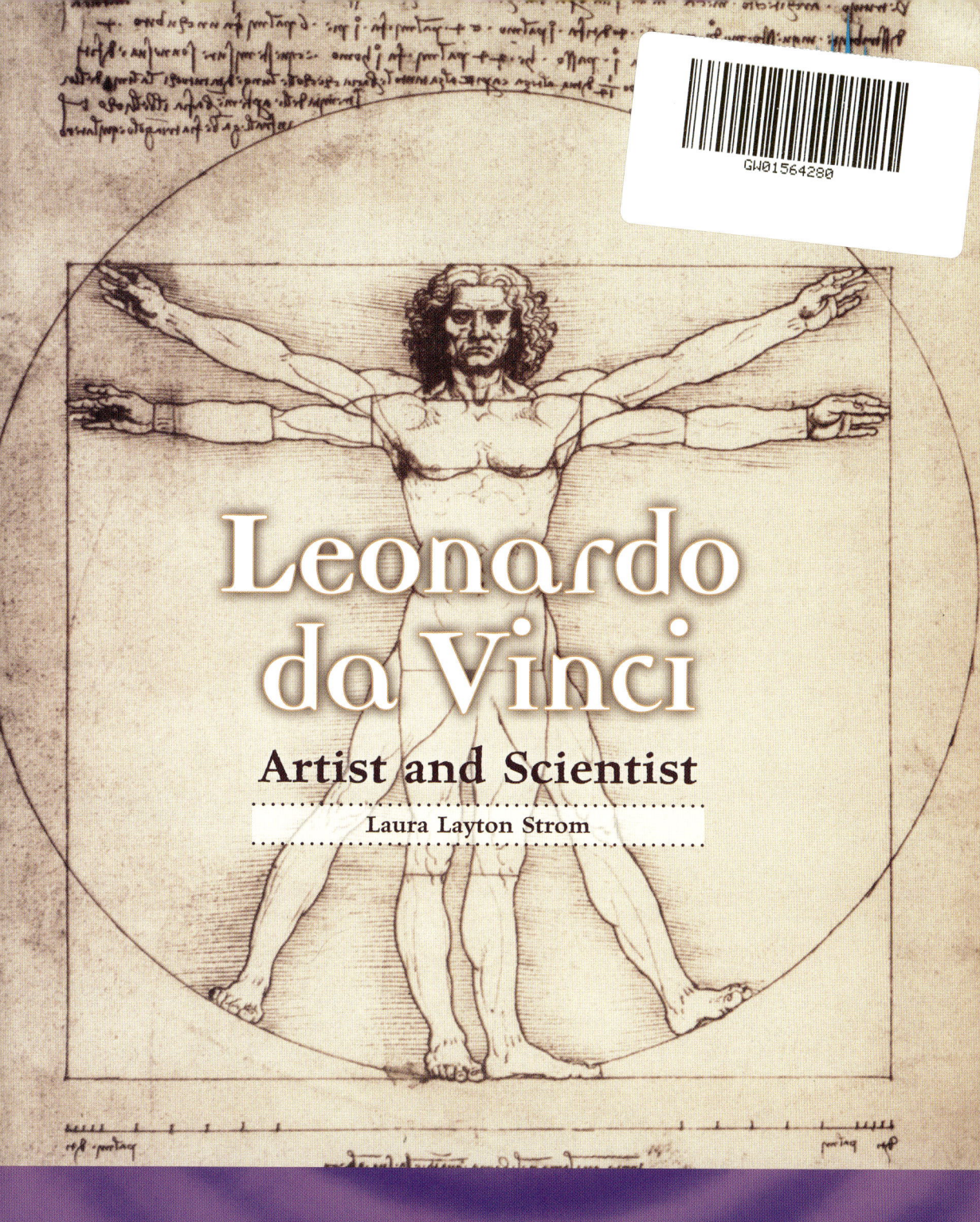

Leonardo da Vinci
Artist and Scientist
Laura Layton Strom

This 2009 British adaptation published by
Scholastic Ltd
Villiers House
Clarendon Avenue
Leamington Spa
Warwickshire CV32 5PR

British Library Cataloguing-in-Publication Data.
A catalogue record for this book is available from the British Library.
ISBN 978-1407-10126-2

© 2009 Weldon Owen Education Limited. All rights reserved.

Author: Laura Layton Strom
Educational Consultants: Ian Morrison and Nikki Gamble
Editors: Mary Atkinson, Marion Archer and Simret Brar
Designer: Matthew Alexander
Photo Researcher: Jamshed Mistry

Photographs by: Getty Images (ad for *The Da Vinci Code* movie); **Jennifer and Brian Lupton** (children, pp. 30–31); **Photolibrary** (cover; crowds at the Louvre, p. 17; p. 20; skeleton studies, p. 21; p. 24; anatomical study, pp. 30–31); **Topfoto: www.stockcentral.co.nz** (p. 25); **Tranz/Corbis** (p. 1; p. 5; pp. 6–16; the *Mona Lisa*, p. 17; pp. 18–19; anatomical study of an arm, p. 21; pp. 22–23; heart diagram, p. 25; pp. 26–28; fantasy drawing, p. 29)

Every effort has been made to trace copyright holders for the works reproduced in this book, and the publishers apologise for any inadvertent omissions.

All illustrations and other photographs © Weldon Owen Education Limited

All rights reserved. This book is sold subject to the condition that it shall not, by way of trade or otherwise, be lent, hired out or otherwise circulated without the publisher's prior consent in any form of binding or cover other than that in which it is published and without a similar condition, including this condition, being imposed upon the subsequent purchaser. No part of this publication may be produced, stored in a retrieval system, or transmitted, in any form or by any means, electronic, mechanical, photocopying, recording or otherwise, other than for the purposes described in the lessons in this book, without the prior permission of the publisher. This book remains in copyright, although permission is granted to copy pages where indicated for classroom distribution and use only in the school which has purchased the book, or by the teacher who has purchased the book, and in accordance with the CLA licensing agreement. Photocopying permission is given only for purchasers and not borrowers of books from any lending service.

Due to the nature of the web, we cannot guarantee the content or links of any site mentioned. We strongly recommend that teachers check websites before using them in the classroom.

Teachers' notes contain extracts from Primary National Strategy's *Primary Framework for Literacy* (2006) www.standards.dfes.gov.uk/primaryframework © Crown copyright. Reproduced under the terms of the Click Use Licence.

1 2 3 4 5 6 7 8 9   9 0 1 2 3 4 5 6 7 8

Printed in China through Colorcraft Ltd., Hong Kong

CONTENTS

HIGH-POWERED WORDS	4
GET ON THE WAVELENGTH	6
Black Death and Bad Blood	8
A Hard Start	10
Early Work	12
War and Sickness	14
Masterpieces	16
The Secret Notebooks	18
The Bodies of the Dead	20
Slimy Eyeballs	22
Water and Wings	24
Leonardo's Last Years	26
Leonardo, Ahead of the Pack	28
AFTERSHOCKS	30
GLOSSARY	32
INDEX	32

HIGH-POWERED WORDS

masterpiece an outstanding work of art or craft

medieval to do with the Middle Ages

Middle Ages the period in European history from about AD 500 to about AD 1500.

perspective the art of drawing or painting a scene so that forms and objects appear to have the same shapes and relative sizes as they do in real life. For example, distant objects are smaller than nearer ones.

Renaissance the period in European history that began in Italy in about 1300 and lasted until about 1600. The Renaissance (meaning "rebirth") was marked by advances in art, literature and science.

....

For easy reference, see Wordmark on back flap.
For additional vocabulary, see Glossary on page 32.

> Medieval — many words have a prefix that give a clue to their meaning. The prefix *medi-* means middle. So medieval is the middle time or middle age. Words with this prefix include *mediocre* — neither good nor bad; *medium* — in the middle position. You may be able to think of some others.

A **perspective** study for *Adoration of the Magi*, an unfinished work by Leonardo da Vinci

Leonardo da Vinci was one of the greatest artists of all time. He was also an early scientist. However, his scientific work was not understood until long after he died.

Leonardo was born in Italy in 1452. He lived at the end of the **Middle Ages**. This was a time when most learning had to do with religion. Leonardo also lived at the beginning of the **Renaissance**. This was when Europeans began to study the world around them. They began to advance ideas in science, art and literature. Leonardo was more of a "Renaissance man" than someone living in the Middle Ages. He passionately questioned why and how things happened.

In Leonardo's time, Italy was not a single country. It was made up of several **city-states**, each with its own government. Leonardo was born in the Florence city-state.

As an artist, Leonardo produced two of the world's best-known paintings: *Mona Lisa* and *The Last Supper*. As a scientist, he made many discoveries and thought up many inventions long before other scientists did. However, he didn't publish his ideas. Perhaps this was because people were not yet ready to accept them.

Detail from *The Last Supper*, by Leonardo da Vinci

Black Death

The Middle Ages were violent and primitive by our standards. People who questioned laws were beaten or killed. Few people owned books or could read. Most people didn't wash often. They didn't understand the need for **hygiene**. City streets were piled with stinking waste. Rats lived in many homes. **Plagues** killed thousands of people. During the black-death **epidemic** of 1348, one in every three people died! Even at other times, most people lived short lives. If diseases didn't kill them, medical treatments did. Patients were sliced open to release "bad blood". Surgery was done by barbers. It often led to death from bleeding, shock or infection.

In the Middle Ages, some people thought that dancing would make God spare them from the plague.

and Bad Blood

SHOCKER

In the Middle Ages, people stuffed pig manure up their noses to stop nose bleeds.

This medieval drawing shows the inside of the body. People's knowledge of the body was based on very little actual examination.

In **medieval** Europe, people did not look for scientific reasons for the things that happened. Bad blood, **supernatural** powers and the stars were said to cause society's ills. Most people accepted these explanations. However, by the 1400s in Italy, things were beginning to change. The Renaissance had begun. Leonardo da Vinci was part of the changes. Leonardo questioned everything!

A Hard Start

The house near Vinci where Leonardo grew up

You can find out more about Leonardo's paintings on The National Gallery website www.nationalgallery.org.uk

Leonardo was born near Vinci, a town in Florence. In fact, the name *da Vinci* means "from Vinci". Leonardo's parents were not married. Leonardo lived with his father's family. He later had several stepmothers and many half brothers and sisters. As he grew up, he spent a lot of time alone. Leonardo always carried a notebook. He enjoyed drawing things he saw in nature.

Leonardo was not allowed to attend university or to work in a top profession. This was because his parents hadn't married. Leonardo didn't let this hold him back. He decided to make up for these unfair rules by reading everything he could. Leonardo's father noticed his son's artistic talent. He helped Leonardo get a lucky break – a job with Andrea del Verrocchio, a master artist.

SHOCKER
When Leonardo's father died, Leonardo's half brothers and sisters divided up his things. They gave Leonardo nothing!

Leonardo was Verrocchio's **apprentice** for ten years. *The Baptism of Christ* was painted mainly by Verrocchio. Leonardo did the angel at the far left.

Is this handsome teenager Leonardo? Most historians think that Leonardo modelled for this statue by Verrocchio.

Early Work

Leonardo studied mathematics as a young artist. This helped him use **perspective** to make his paintings look realistic. Leonardo also **dissected** animals to learn more about their structures. For fun, he sometimes joined body parts from different animals into creepy combinations, such as lizard-bats. Verrocchio encouraged dissection among his apprentices. He wanted complete accuracy in their work. He also encouraged them to make plaster casts of their own body parts and of corpse body parts. The apprentices used them to help make realistic sculptures.

Leonardo always preferred sketching ideas to finishing his artworks.

Louis I, Duke of Anjou, by Johansen Krause, 1300s

Leonardo's *Lady With an Ermine*, 1480s

SHOCKER
Leonardo liked to put bits of dead animals in other artists' equipment to shock them.

The portrait on the left is from the Middle Ages. The one on the right is an example of Renaissance art. Which one seems more realistic? Why do you think this is?

Leonardo worked hard, but rarely finished his work. He toyed with designs for new machines. Leonardo was easily distracted. He jumped from project to project. Historians say Leonardo left behind more unfinished work than any other artist.

Leonardo was disorganised and messy. He had trouble concentrating on one thing for long. However, he was quick-minded and had a wonderful imagination. He was also curious, sensitive and polite.

War and

When Leonardo finished his training, he needed to find work. Since the Italian city-states were at war, he decided that designing war machines might be a good bet. He later came to despise war. However, at this stage, the challenge of designing war machines excited him. He designed guns, submarines and many other things. They were far ahead of their time, but most were never built.

In 1481, Leonardo was passed over as an artist for the Sistine Chapel in Rome. Angry that the **Pope** had not chosen him for this **prestigious** job, he decided it was time for a change. In 1482, he moved to Milan. There he got a job as a military engineer and architect.

The black death led Leonardo to study hygiene and **sanitation**. Italy's city streets were filled with human waste. Leonardo concluded that waste carries diseases into drinking water. He made a plan for a healthy city. It had plumbing, street cleaning and public toilets.

What else can you find out about Leonardo's inventions? You might like to read Andrew Langley's *Eyewitness: Leonardo da Vinci* or Thomas Brezina's *Who Can Crack the Leonardo da Vinci Code?*

Leonardo had a sense of humour. He was fascinated by unusual features as well as beautiful ones.

Sickness

Some of Leonardo's designs for war machines, including a "tank"

SHOCKER
The plague struck Milan in 1484. More than 10,000 people died. With so many dead, not everyone could be buried right away. Many bodies were left to be gnawed on by rats.

The plague struck Italy many times during the Middle Ages and Renaissance. Leonardo, however, escaped the disease.

Masterpieces

In 1495, Leonardo began a project now considered a **masterpiece**. It was *The Last Supper*. He painted this giant mural on the walls of a **monastery** dining hall. He painted for days at a time. Sometimes he forgot to eat. Leonardo used a new method of painting that he had invented himself. Unfortunately, the paint soon began to flake off. Experts have worked to keep the painting visible. But, sadly, not much of the original paint remains.

Recap
The Last Supper:
- is a masterpiece
- is a giant mural
- used a new painting method
- is in poor condition

The Last Supper

Teacher Notes
Jolt your children into content-area reading success!

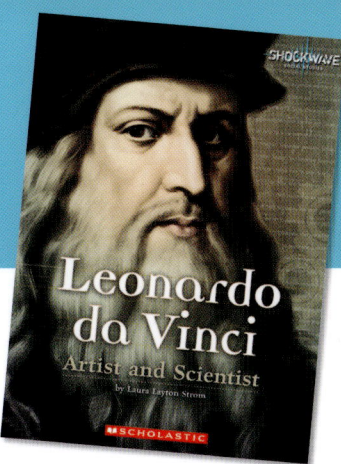

Synopsis
Leonardo da Vinci explores the scientific and artistic accomplishments of da Vinci. The text highlights how far ahead of his time Leonardo was, and how science and art can mix to produce some remarkable results.

Vocabulary Development
Read and discuss the high-powered words on page 4 prior to reading the book.
The high-powered words for this book are:
masterpiece, medieval, Middle Ages, perspective, Renaissance.

Reading Assessment Focus
Retrieve, select and describe information, events or ideas from texts and use quotations and reference to text:
- identify generalisation in texts and supporting statements
- summarise information by identifying the main points and organising information.

Before Reading – Get on the Wavelength
- Invite the children to discuss any artists or scientists they may be familiar with.
  Ask: *What are some of the traits that are typical of both scientists and artists?*
  Have them discuss their responses. Then read the questions on the back cover. Invite the children to discuss any information they may have about Leonardo da Vinci.
- Discuss the **Word Stunner**. Talk about the Contents page and how it is arranged. Help the children understand that the main body of the text is located between the featured lines.

SHOCKER
The plague struck Milan in 1484. More than 10,000 people died. With so many dead, not everyone could be buried right away. Many bodies were left to be gnawed on by rats.

Develop Reading Strategies

Monitor the reading behaviour of individual children. Encourage the children to think about their own reading behaviour and the strategies they use when they encounter difficulties. Use opportunities to help the children employ a combination of semantic, syntactic and graphophonic cues to anticipate text and check predictions. Encourage them to re-read text to confirm and to gain further information.

Discuss the five icons on the cover flap. These icons are designed to help the children find out more about the topic, the different ways information may be presented and how to develop the skills necessary to be a successful reader.

Pages	Guiding the Reading	Text and Visual Features	Observation and Assessment
6–7	Read and discuss these pages with the children. **Ask:** *Why do you think Leonardo was considered a genius?*	Help the children read and interpret the map on page 7.	Are the children able to form and justify an opinion about Leonardo?
8–9	Have the children read these pages and discuss some of the similarities and differences between now and the Middle Ages.	Discuss the use of the **Shocker**. **Ask:** *Why do you think the author has included this "shocking" information?*	Are the children able to compare and contrast aspects of the Middle Ages and modern times?
10–13	**Ask:** *What do you think life was like for Leonardo as he was growing up?* Have the children respond, read and discuss.	**Ask:** *What does the heading suggest the passage will be about?* Draw attention to the use of headings to help make reading easier.	Are the children able to form an appropriate generalisation about Leonardo's early life?

Leonardo da Vinci
Laura Layton Strom

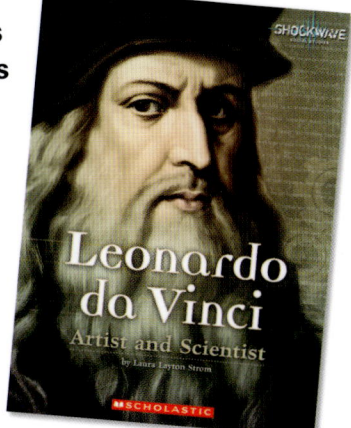

FACT FILE

Here's a quick summary of some of the facts from the book. Use these questions and answers to test your understanding, to stump your friends or as an outline for further research.

What caused the deaths of a third of the entire population in 1348?
A disease called the black death caused them.

Why wasn't Leonardo allowed to attend university?
His parents had not married.

What was so unusual about the way Leonardo wrote in his notebooks?
He wrote in mirror writing.

What did Leonardo discover by studying animals' eyes?
He discovered that animals that feed at night have larger eyes than brains.

Leonardo had a theory about rivers that was completely wrong. What was it?
He thought that rivers had a heart that pumped water.

Why did Leonardo's work doing autopsies make him unpopular?
Some people thought this meant that he was involved in witchcraft.

What does Leonardo's *Vitruvian Man* show?
It shows the proportions of the human body: the span of a person's arms is equal to his or her height.

FACT FILE

Think Tank
Write a summary sentence for each heading. The first one is done for you.

Heading	Summary Sentence
A Hard Start	Leonardo had a difficult early life.
Early Work	
War and Sickness	
Masterpieces	
The Secret Notebooks	
The Bodies of the Dead	
Slimy Eyeballs	
Water and Wings	

Word Power
In the word *telescope, tele* means "at a distance", and *scope* means "to perceive" (see or hear). Find the meanings of these other "scope" words. Use a dictionary or other reference source if necessary.

oscilloscope _____

stethoscope _____

microscope _____

periscope _____

Writer's Workshop
The recap box on page 25 shows how a generalisation is formed. Write three points in favour of the following generalisation:

Life is better now than in the fifteenth century.

-
-
-

Pages	Guiding the Reading	Text and Visual Features	Observation and Assessment
14–15	**Say:** *Read pages 14–15 to find out how da Vinci became interested in health issues.* Discuss da Vinci's interest in sanitation and relate it to current health issues.	Read sentence one of the second paragraph. Ask what "passed over" means. Tell them to read the next sentence to look for clues ("not chosen"). Emphasise the importance of reading on.	Are the children able to recall and discuss Leonardo's interest in hygiene and sanitation?
16–17	Invite the children to read these pages and discuss these "masterpieces". **Ask:** *Which do you think is the most impressive? Why?*	Highlight the **Quick Recap**. Point out that it is a way of summarising information. Ask them when it might be useful to use a recap.	Are the children able to form and justify an opinion about these masterpieces?
18–21	Have the children read these pages and discuss Leonardo's extensive use of notebooks. Invite them to talk about his interest in the human body.	Discuss the **Shocker** on page 21. Ask children to suggest what they know about decay. **Ask:** *What methods are used to prevent or slow decay?*	Are the children able to discuss aspects of Leonardo's interest in the human body and dissection?
22–25	**Say:** *Read to the end of page 25. Find out what else interested da Vinci.* When the children have finished, have them talk about his fascination with water and flying.	Discuss the **Quick Recap** on page 25. Explain that it is a generalisation with supporting statements. This technique can be used to identify evidence to support an argument.	Do the children display an understanding of Leonardo's fascination with water and flying?
26–29	Have the children read these pages and discuss the reasons Leonardo was considered ahead of his time.	Have the children talk about Leonardo's last drawings. **Ask:** *What do you think these drawings represent?*	Are the children able to recall and discuss some of Leonardo's major innovations?
30–31	Invite the children to read these pages and discuss their personal opinions.	Invite the children to visit the highlighted website to find out more.	Are the children able to form and justify an opinion?

Provide time for the children to re-read the book on their own or with a partner.

Aftershocks

Fluency

Some children continue to read word by word, even when the text is within their capabilities. This habituated response can be difficult to break. One way of speeding up the reading is by using a masking card. Select a page. Read it together a few times, until the children become familiar with the content. Then, as the child reads aloud, move a blank note card across the page, following the text from left to right at a steady, slightly accelerated pace. This technique encourages the eye to move more quickly. Repeat this several times. Then remove the card and have the child read the text again.

Comprehension

Invite the children to find examples of Leonardo da Vinci's accomplishments in different areas of interest. Use a chart to note their suggestions and use this to prompt discussion about more recent achievements in these areas.

Areas of Interest	Accomplishments
science	
art	
medicine	
flight	

Vocabulary and Language

Have the children re-read the **Word Stunner** on page 21, and discuss other prefixes used to create opposites. In pairs, challenge the children to list as many words as possible. Ask pairs to share their lists and use dictionaries to find further examples.

ir	il	im	in	un	dis
irresponsible	illegal	impossible	injustice	unfair	disengage

Writing

Discuss the chart of da Vinci's accomplishments in different areas. Invite the children to choose the accomplishment they find most impressive and explain their choice. Have them use high-powered and glossary words.

Leonardo da Vinci
Laura Layton Strom

FACT FILE

Here's a quick summary of some of the facts from the book. Use these questions and answers to test your understanding, to stump your friends or as an outline for further research.

What caused the deaths of a third of the entire population in 1348?
A disease called the black death caused them.

Why wasn't Leonardo allowed to attend university?
His parents had not married.

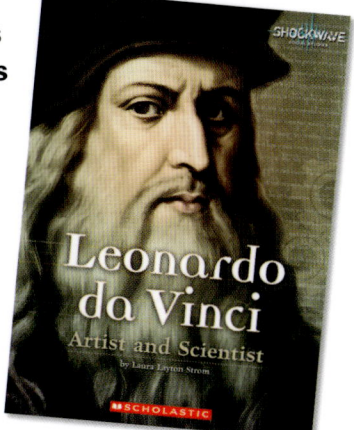

What was so unusual about the way Leonardo wrote in his notebooks?
He wrote in mirror writing.

What did Leonardo discover by studying animals' eyes?
He discovered that animals that feed at night have larger eyes than brains.

Leonardo had a theory about rivers that was completely wrong. What was it?
He thought that rivers had a heart that pumped water.

Why did Leonardo's work doing autopsies make him unpopular?
Some people thought this meant that he was involved in witchcraft.

What does Leonardo's *Vitruvian Man* show?
It shows the proportions of the human body: the span of a person's arms is equal to his or her height.

FACT FILE

Think Tank

Write a summary sentence for each heading. The first one is done for you.

Heading	Summary Sentence
A Hard Start	Leonardo had a difficult early life.
Early Work	
War and Sickness	
Masterpieces	
The Secret Notebooks	
The Bodies of the Dead	
Slimy Eyeballs	
Water and Wings	

Word Power

In the word *telescope*, *tele* means "at a distance", and *scope* means "to perceive" (see or hear). Find the meanings of these other "scope" words. Use a dictionary or other reference source if necessary.

oscilloscope _____

stethoscope _____

microscope _____

periscope _____

Writer's Workshop

The recap box on page 25 shows how a generalisation is formed. Write three points in favour of the following generalisation:

Life is better now than in the fifteenth century.

-
-
-

Leonardo da Vinci
Laura Layton Strom

FACT FILE

Here's a quick summary of some of the facts from the book. Use these questions and answers to test your understanding, to stump your friends or as an outline for further research.

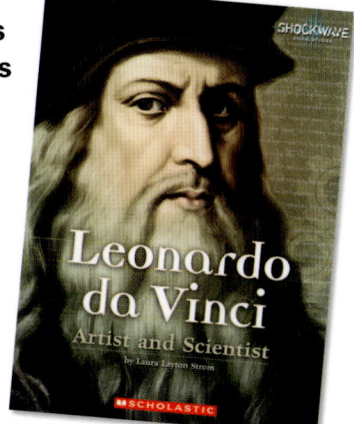

What caused the deaths of a third of the entire population in 1348?
A disease called the black death caused them.

Why wasn't Leonardo allowed to attend university?
His parents had not married.

What was so unusual about the way Leonardo wrote in his notebooks?
He wrote in mirror writing.

What did Leonardo discover by studying animals' eyes?
He discovered that animals that feed at night have larger eyes than brains.

Leonardo had a theory about rivers that was completely wrong. What was it?
He thought that rivers had a heart that pumped water.

Why did Leonardo's work doing autopsies make him unpopular?
Some people thought this meant that he was involved in witchcraft.

What does Leonardo's *Vitruvian Man* show?
It shows the proportions of the human body: the span of a person's arms is equal to his or her height.

Think Tank

Write a summary sentence for each heading. The first one is done for you.

Heading	Summary Sentence
A Hard Start	Leonardo had a difficult early life.
Early Work	
War and Sickness	
Masterpieces	
The Secret Notebooks	
The Bodies of the Dead	
Slimy Eyeballs	
Water and Wings	

Word Power

In the word *telescope, tele* means "at a distance", and *scope* means "to perceive" (see or hear). Find the meanings of these other "scope" words. Use a dictionary or other reference source if necessary.

oscilloscope _____

stethoscope _____

microscope _____

periscope _____

Writer's Workshop

The recap box on page 25 shows how a generalisation is formed. Write three points in favour of the following generalisation:

Life is better now than in the fifteenth century.

-
-
-

FACT FILE

In 1503, Leonardo created another masterpiece – *Mona Lisa*. The woman in the painting has an unusual, irregular smile. The smile has intrigued people ever since it was first painted. The painting must have been very special to Leonardo. He kept it near him for the rest of his life.

Mona Lisa

SHOCKER
No one knows for sure who posed for *Mona Lisa*. Some people have suggested that it was Leonardo himself!

When Leonardo died, his apprentice, Salai, inherited *Mona Lisa*. When Salai died in 1523, *Mona Lisa* was bought by the French king. It is now in the Louvre, a museum in Paris. There it attracts large crowds every day.

The Secret Notebooks

Leonardo often wondered about things that others took for granted. Why is the sky blue? What causes vomiting? How do birds fly? Sometimes he tested his ideas. He wrote down his predictions, did experiments and then wrote conclusions. This was an early use of what later developed into the **scientific method**.

Leonardo often wrote in **mirror writing**. This may have been because he was left-handed. Writing from right to left made it easier not to smudge the ink. When he wanted to keep something secret, he wrote in code.

Leonardo's surviving notes have been divided into 10 books called codices. In 1994, Microsoft founder Bill Gates bought one for £20.5 million! It contains Leonardo's notes on topics such as water, gravity and light.

Leonardo's *Vitruvian Man* shows the proportions of the human body. It shows that the span of a person's arms is equal to his or her height.

Leonardo's drawing of a **siphon** looks surprisingly like a modern shower head.

Leonardo jotted down every **theory**, design and idea that came into his head. Often he wrote through the night. His notebooks became his reason for living. Sadly, the people who later inherited the notebooks didn't realise what they had. They lost about three-quarters of them! Most of the 13,000 surviving pages went unread for years.

The Bodies of the Dead

Leonardo kept much of his scientific work private. He may have worried about being laughed at, or worse, being thrown into prison. The dissection work he did was illegal. Because of this, Leonardo worked at night. Historians think that he dissected more than 30 bodies, mostly of criminals. Leonardo believed that the human body was the ultimate machine. He wanted to know how the skeleton linked up. He wanted to know how blood flowed, and how muscles worked. He was the first person to:
- explain the skeletal system correctly
- discover hardened **arteries** as a cause of death
- report that the heart is a muscle that pumps blood
- draw a human baby inside its mother's body.

SHOCKER

In the 15th century, neither refrigeration nor chemical preservatives existed. Bodies decayed quickly. Leonardo had to work fast or risk throwing up from the stink.

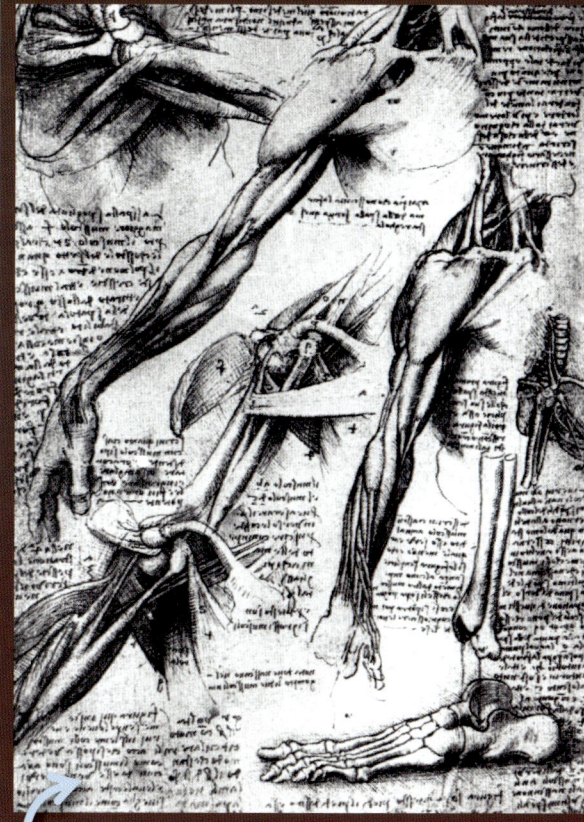

Leonardo sketched the body parts he studied, including muscles (above) and bones (right). His drawings look more like modern medical drawings than medieval ones (see page 9).

The *il-* prefix is used to form opposites: legal/illegal, logical/illogical.

Slimy Eyeballs

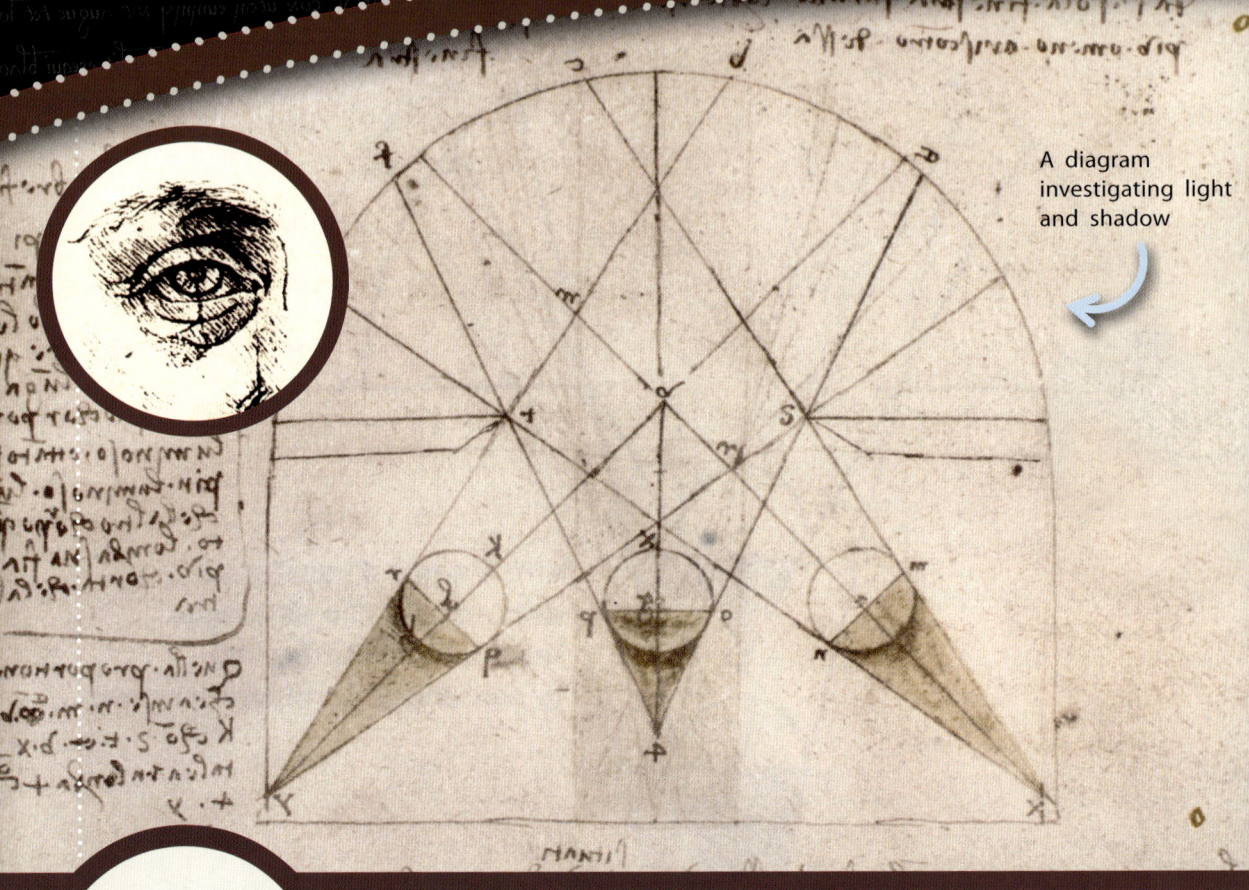

A diagram investigating light and shadow

Most people in Leonardo's time accepted the theories of the ancient Greeks. Some of the ancient Greeks had written that the eye sends light rays to the objects it sees. Leonardo, however, questioned these theories. He was fascinated with eyes and vision. He made models with mirrors, glass balls and lenses to figure out how the eye works. He even discussed the idea of contact lenses.

SHOCKER

To study eyeballs more easily, Leonardo needed to make them easier to cut. He hard-boiled them like eggs. This made them less slimy and mushy.

Leonardo studied light, reflection and shadows in great detail. He designed a device for viewing a solar eclipse safely. He also wrote about the idea of using mirrors and lenses to magnify the moon and planets. Yet the first telescope was not invented until a century later.

Leonardo also studied animals' eyes. He realised that animals that feed at night have larger eyes than brains. Other land animals usually have smaller eyes than brains.

Water and Wings

Water fascinated Leonardo. He made notes about it and about how to control it. He made drawings of watercraft and diving suits. He even made plans for very wide, flat shoes that could be used to walk on water.

Leonardo yearned to fly. He had learned to swim by copying frogs. So he tried to fly by studying birds, bats and flying insects. He designed many different flying machines. Historians disagree as to whether he actually made any of them. Although some were well designed, they were too heavy to actually fly. However, Leonardo is credited with designing the first parachute.

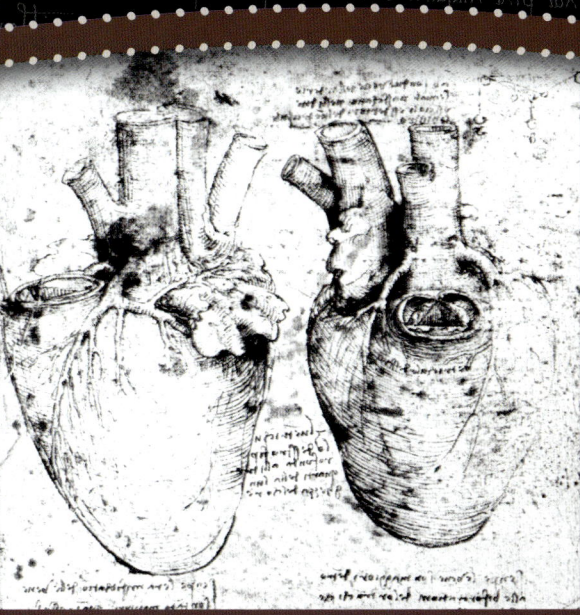

Leonardo was very interested in water. He:
- learned to swim by copying frogs
- made plans for shoes to walk on water
- made notes about controlling water
- drew watercraft and diving suits

Not all of Leonardo's theories were completely correct. For example, he rightly said that the heart pumps blood through the body. However, he wrongly concluded that rivers contain a heart that pumps water!

Leonardo drew this sketch of his idea for a life jacket.

Some of these innovations were first dreamed up by Leonardo but never published by him.

- Steam power, 1698
- Parachute, 1783
- Bicycle, 1790
- Helicopter, 1907
- Robot, 1921
- Solar panels, 1954

Leonardo's Last

By 1500, Leonardo had spent so much time on his notebooks that he had little money. He began moving from town to town, taking on paying jobs. He mostly designed machines, gardens, home improvements and toys. Sometimes he was hired to draw maps.

In his later years, Leonardo moved to Rome to work for the Pope. When he wasn't working, he studied plants in the beautiful Vatican gardens. He was also allowed to do **autopsies** on those who died at the local hospital. However, this work made him unpopular. Some people thought it meant he was involved in witchcraft.

Years

Find out more about Leonardo da Vinci at the Clos Luce website
www.vinci-closluce.com

Leonardo da Vinci once lived in this French manor house, which now houses a museum.

Leonardo's last job took him to France. He became Premier Painter, Engineer and Architect for King Francis I. He worked until his eyesight failed, his teeth fell out and he became paralysed by a stroke. In 1519, he died. He was 67-years-old.

Some of Leonardo's last drawings were nightmarish pictures of the end of the world. Psychiatrists think he knew that he was close to death and was fearful of it.

27

Leonardo,

Leonardo left behind astonishing drawings and paintings. He also described scientific ideas and inventions far beyond anything others were producing at that time. Here are a few of his many ideas that others later improved or invented themselves.

- The first accurate drawings of anatomy.
  These are credited to Dr Andreas Vesalius (1543).

- The theory that the earth revolves around the sun.
  This is credited to astronomer Nicolaus Copernicus (1543).

- The law that states that objects at rest tend to remain at rest, originally called Leonardo's Law. Today, we call this Newton's first law of motion. Scientist Isaac Newton published the law nearly 200 years later, in 1687.

- Flying machines.
  These are credited to the Wright Brothers (1903).

This bicycle design of Leonardo's is nearly identical to one "invented" in about 1885.

Ahead of the Pack

Some of Leonardo's drawings came mainly from his imagination.

Today, many people assume that science and art cannot mix. They think that a person is either good at science and mathematics or good at creative subjects. Leonardo is proof that works of great genius can emerge from the combination of art and science.

Many people have been inspired by Leonardo. *The Da Vinci Code* is a best-selling novel by Dan Brown. It has also been made into a film. In the story, someone is murdered. The body is posed like Leonardo's *Vitruvian Man*. The paintings *Mona Lisa* and *The Last Supper* supposedly contain clues to solving the crime.

AFTERSHOCKS

Leonardo loved nature. He studied it with awe and with a scientific mind. He was a vegetarian in a time when almost everyone ate meat. He believed that all creatures that moved felt pain. He even despised hunting. However, Leonardo also cut up dead bodies to study them, which was against the law.

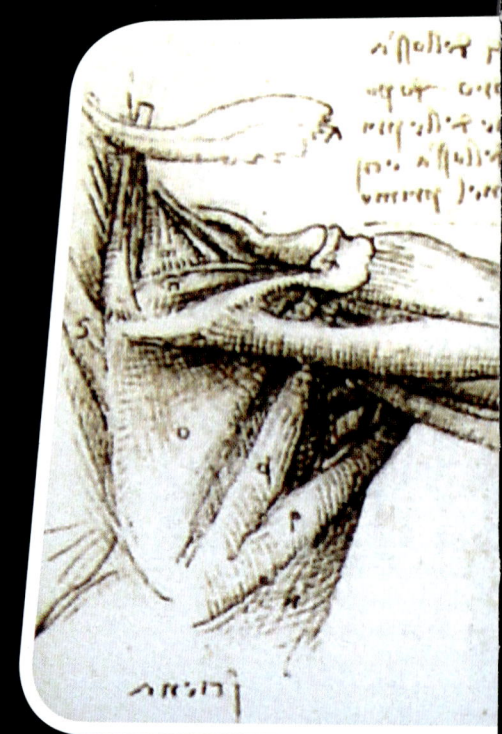

WHAT DO YOU THINK?

Do you think Leonardo was right to cut up bodies illegally?

PRO

Leonardo had to break the law. There was no other way he could learn about the body. The people were dead, so they felt no pain. He was doing important work that improved his art. It also could have improved medicine if he had published his work.

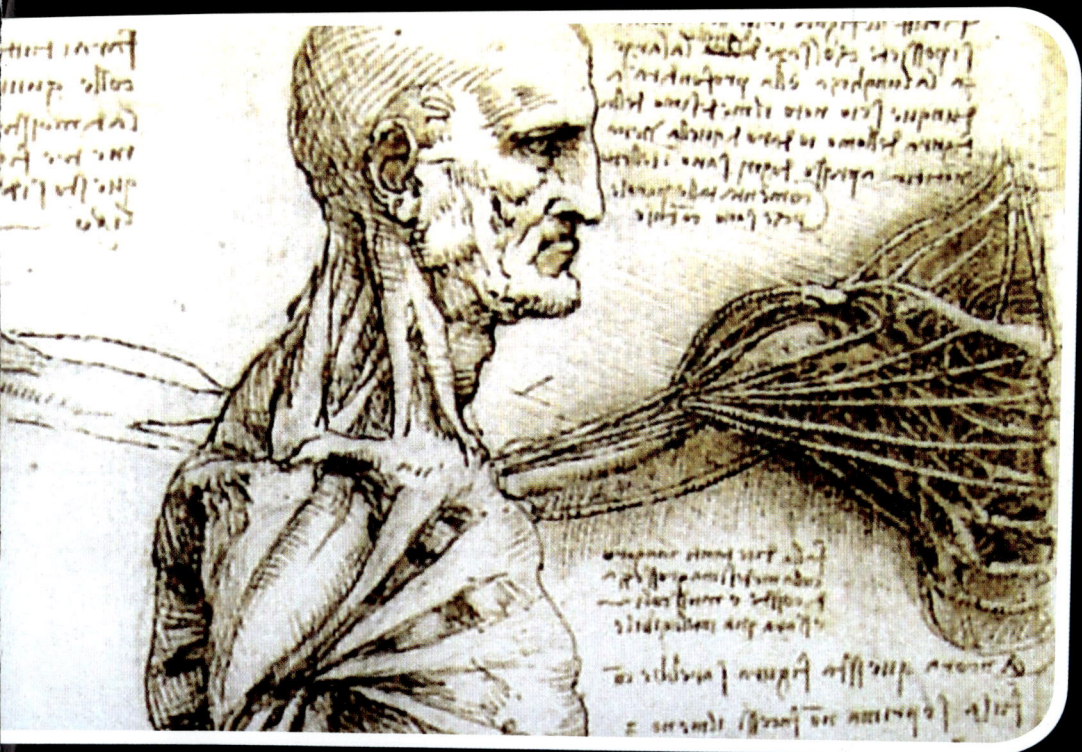

CON

I think it was disrespectful and disgusting. The people had not given permission for him to do that work. It was illegal, and laws are made for a reason. If people could take dead bodies anytime, there would be less respect for the dead.

Leonardo da Vinci was a fascinating person. Go to **www.mos.org/leonardo/index.html** to learn more about him.

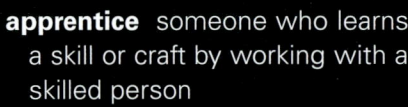

GLOSSARY

apprentice someone who learns a skill or craft by working with a skilled person

artery a blood vessel that carries blood away from the heart

autopsy the study of a body to work out the cause of death

city-state a city and its surrounding area that functions like a nation with its own government

dissect to cut the tissue of an organism in order to study its structure

epidemic a disease that spreads quickly

hygiene conditions and practices that improve health and cleanliness

mirror writing writing that reads from right to left and has letters that face the wrong way. Mirror writing looks like ordinary writing in a mirror.

monastery a place where monks live and work

plague a disease, especially the black death, or bubonic plague, that spreads quickly and kills many people

Pope the leader of the Roman Catholic Church

prestigious something that brings respect and high status

sanitation systems for keeping water clean and getting rid of sewage

scientific method a way of gaining scientific knowledge by observing, experimenting and analysing results

siphon a bent tube through which water can be made to flow

supernatural to do with things that cannot be described with natural laws or normal understanding

superstitious a belief in supernatural things, such as witchcraft

theory an idea about why something happens

INDEX

anatomy	9, 20–21, 28
dissection	12–13, 20–21, 30
drawings (by Leonardo)	5, 12, 14–15, 18–22, 24–25, 27, 29–31
eyes	22–23
flight	18, 24, 28
hygiene	8, 14
Italy	6–7, 9–10, 14–15
Last Supper, The	7, 16, 29
light	19, 22–23
Louvre, the	17
Middle Ages	6, 8–9, 13, 15, 27
mirror writing	18
Mona Lisa	7, 17, 29
muscles	20–21
paintings (by Leonardo)	6–7, 11, 13, 16–17
plague (black death)	8, 14–15
Renaissance	6, 9, 13, 15
science	6–7, 9, 18–25, 28–30
vegetarianism	30
Verrocchio, Andrea del	10–12
Vinci	10
Vitruvian Man	19, 29
war machines	14–15
water	14, 19, 24–25